Reinvent Your Reality

**The ultimate guide
Unleash your full
Potential**

K06 Editions

"

This book is an extraordinary guide
that captivated me from the first page.
What I appreciate the most is the
unique structure of the independent
chapters, offering a rare flexibility in
my reading. I can choose to dive into
Chapter 4 when I need to light my way
to new perspectives, or immerse
myself in Chapter 7 when I want to
connect to the positive impact I can
have in the world. . I don't need to read
the whole book. Each chapter is a
nugget of wisdom, and this book has
become my daily thoughtful
companion. I recommend it to anyone
looking to reinvent their reality at their
own pace.

Bryann Cott, Journalist *THE VOICE* , [2011-2022]

K06 Editions

Reinvent Your Reality

ABOUT THE AUTHOR

Born in Togo in 1987, Kossi Ntiafalali Aziagba is considered the pillar of a silent immigrant revolution that aims to end what he calls "modern slavery". As an immigrant himself, he denounces the torture and autocracy of African leaders, especially in his country of origin. He denounces the mistreatment of immigrants and asylum seekers, censorships and the use of refugee camps as a new channel for the exploitation of migrants and black people.

© 2023, KOSSI NTIAFALALI AZIAGBA

Reference Author: www.aziagba.com

K06 Editions

Reinvent Your Reality

The Ultimate Guide to Unlocking Your Full Potential

Chapitre 1
Awakening to Possibilities

Every morning we get up to start a new day.

- What if we approached each day as an opportunity to redefine our reality?

Welcome to this journey of transformation and personal growth.

This guide was designed to help you discover the endless possibilities that reside within you and unleash your full potential.

In this chapter, we will explore the foundations of self-reinvention and how to embrace the transformative potential that resides in every moment.

We'll dive into the key concepts that will be explored throughout this book, laying the groundwork for your own journey to a fulfilling and enlightening reality.

Together, we'll explore how you can broaden your horizons, adopt an open-to-opportunity mindset, and learn to see the world around you with new brilliance.

Prepare to discover a renewed vision of yourself and what you can achieve.

Each morning the sun rises, brightening a new day and with it, new opportunities.

- How can we fully exploit these opportunities to reinvent our reality and unleash our full potential?

This first chapter serves as a springboard for your personal journey of transformation.

You will discover how every moment, every breath, offers the possibility of creating a reality that resonates with your deepest aspirations.

The Web of Reality

Imagine reality as a complex, infinitely woven web.

Each thread represents a possibility, an experience, a decision you can make.

This weaving represents the fabric of your life.

You have the power to choose the threads you weave, add new colors and create a unique pattern that reflects your true essence.

- But how do you deliberately weave this web to create the reality you desire?

✦ Awaken Consciousness

The first step to reinventing your reality is to awaken to the multitude of possibilities that surround you. It means becoming aware of your thoughts, emotions, and actions.

Too often, we get carried away by routine and habits, letting opportunities pass us by without seizing them. By becoming aware, you can begin to identify the thought patterns that are limiting you and open the door to new insights.

✦ Journey to the Unknown

Awakening to new possibilities also requires the courage to venture into the unknown.
Imagine yourself standing at the edge of a cliff, ready to dive into the deep waters of the unknown.
The unknown may seem daunting, but that's where the most exciting opportunities lie.

✦ An Invitation to Transformation

As you embark on this journey of personal reinvention, consider each chapter as an invitation to explore a different side of yourself.

Every page you turn, every exercise you perform brings you closer to the reality you have the potential to create.

Reinvent Every Day

Guide 1: Cultivate an Opportunity Mentality

Every day is a blank canvas on which you can paint your aspirations. In this first guide, we'll explore how to cultivate an opportunity mindset to redefine your daily reality.

Every day gives us a fresh start. Each day is like a chance to shape your reality according to your desires. Learn to approach each morning with an open mind and clear intention.

1. Set Your Morning Intention

Start each day by setting a clear intention. It could be an emotion you want to feel, a goal you want to achieve, or a quality you want to embody. For example, set the intention to "cultivate gratitude" for the day.

2. Practice Gratitude

Gratitude is a powerful way to reinvent your reality. Each morning, take a few moments to list three things for which you are grateful.
It can be as simple as the sun shining or a smile from a loved one.

3. Explore the Unknown

Every day offers opportunities for exploration. Try something new, even if it's small.
It could be a new route for your morning run or try a dish you've never tasted before.
These little explorations expand your reality.

4. Engage in Authentic Conversations

Every interaction with others is an opportunity to reinvent your social reality. Engage in authentic conversations, ask deep questions, and really listen to the answers.

You might connect with someone in ways you never imagined.

5. Find Beauty in Small Things

Redefining your reality also means seeing the beauty in the details. Observe the small moments of joy - a blooming flower, the laughter of a child, the taste of a cup of coffee.

These moments add depth to your daily experience.

6. Reflect and Adjust

At the end of the day, take a few moments to reflect on the highlights of your day. What did you learn ?

What did you like? What would you have done differently? Use these thoughts to adjust your approach the next day.

Each sunrise is an invitation to redefine your reality.

By cultivating an opportunity mentality, you will turn your days into meaningful and fulfilling experiences.

Use this guide to approach each day with a renewed sense of discovery and possibility.

Practical and Technical Tips for Reinventing Every Day:

- **Morning Journaling:** Start each morning by writing in a journal. Write down your intentions for the day, your goals, and what you are grateful for. This practice helps clarify your thoughts and create a positive outlook.

Daily Meditation: Allow yourself a few minutes for meditation. Close your eyes, take a deep breath, and center yourself.

This helps you create a mindset conducive to openness to new opportunities.

Daily Challenges: Each day, set yourself a small challenge. It could be striking up a conversation with a stranger, exploring a new hobby, or getting out of your usual routine.

Creative Planning: Plan your day creatively. Use colors, icons or symbols to represent your tasks and joyful moments. It gives a dynamic perspective to your day.

Reflection Time: Set aside time at the end of the day to reflect on your experiences. Ask yourself questions like "What did I learn today?" and "How can I improve tomorrow?"

Mindfulness Practice: Practice mindfulness throughout the day. Focus on how you feel during common activities like eating, walking, or listening to music.

Moments of Gratitude: Create moments of gratitude.

Each time you wait, mentally write down three things you are grateful for. This reinforces positivity in your day.

Positive Bedtime Ritual: Before sleeping, reflect on three positive times of the day. It will help you fall asleep with an optimistic outlook and set the stage for the next day.

Acts of Kindness: Perform an act of kindness every day.

It could be a simple action like a warm smile, a sincere compliment, or helping someone in need.

Creative Visualization: Before starting your day, take a few moments to visualize how you want the day to unfold. Picture yourself approaching challenges with confidence and achieving your goals.

Incorporate these tips into your daily routine to redefine each day as an opportunity for personal growth and positive transformation.

Testimony

Every morning I woke up with the same routine. The alarm clock rang, I got up, prepared breakfast and set off for a day full of tasks and obligations.

For a long time, my days seemed to melt into each other, with no real meaning or passion. I felt like I was navigating in an endless fog, far from my dreams and aspirations.

One day, everything changed. I decided to practice a new approach every day. I started by setting a morning intention, asking myself how I could make my day more meaningful.

I found that these intentions gave me a clear direction and a tangible goal to pursue.

By practicing daily meditation, I have found a moment to connect with myself, my aspirations and my emotions.

This practice allowed me to create an inner space to welcome new ideas and opportunities. I started waking up with a sense of anticipation, curious to know what the day would hold.

One of the most powerful moments was when I started setting up daily challenges.

They encouraged me to step out of my comfort zone, explore new experiences, and overcome my fears. Every little challenge I overcame gave me a sense of accomplishment and boosted my self-confidence.

Over time, I realized that I could find beauty in the simplest details of life.
I began to enjoy the flavor of each meal, the warmth of the sun on my skin, and the smiles shared with others.
My daily reality has been transformed into a series of rich and profound experiences.
The practice of gratitude has been the cement of my transformation.

By taking a few moments to acknowledge what I was grateful for, I cultivated a sense of contentment and inner joy.

I realized that reimagining my reality began with acknowledging what I already had.

Today I wake up with joyous anticipation for each new day.

I learned to approach every challenge as an opportunity for growth and every encounter as an opportunity for authentic connection.

By redefining my daily reality, I discovered a renewed sense of passion, purpose and fulfillment.

Every day has become a blank canvas on which I paint my own life masterpiece.

The Foundations of Self-Reinvention:

Embracing the Potential for Transformation

At the heart of every human being is an unlimited potential for transformation.

We have the ability to shape our reality, transcend our limitations, and thrive in ways beyond our imagination.

In this chapter, we'll dive into the basics of self-reinvention and discover how to embrace the transformative potential that resides in every moment.

✦ The Changing Nature of Life

Life itself is constantly changing. The seasons change, the days pass and we grow. However, it is often easy to get stuck in our familiar habits and patterns.

Self-reinvention begins with recognizing that transformation is natural and inevitable.

By embracing this changing nature, we can become active artisans of our own evolution.

⬥ The Power of the Present Moment

The present moment is the anchor point of all transformation. This is where choices are made, actions are taken and decisions are made.
By fully embracing the present moment, we unleash the transformative potential that resides within us.

> *Each moment offers an opportunity*
> *to deliberately choose our thoughts,*
> *emotions, and actions, thereby*
> *shaping our future reality.*

⬥ The Art of Self-Reflection

Self-reinvention begins with self-knowledge. Self -reflection is a powerful tool that allows us to explore our deepest values, beliefs and aspirations.

By taking the time to get to know each other intimately, we open the door to authentic and meaningful transformation.

Each moment of self-reflection is an invitation to reinvent the parts of ourselves that no longer resonate with our highest vision.

⧫ Cultivate Choice Consciousness

We are the creators of our experiences. Every choice we make, whether big or small, influences our reality.

Cultivating choice awareness means recognizing that we have the power to decide how to respond to life circumstances.

By embracing this awareness, we can begin to deliberately choose thoughts, emotions, and actions that support our transformation.

⧫ Transformation in Action

Self-reinvention is not a passive concept, but a series of intentional actions.

Every small step we take towards our goals and aspirations is a step towards transformation.

Whether it's developing new skills, letting go of limiting habits, or taking calculated risks, every action matters.

By exploring these foundations, we lay the groundwork for our journey of reinvention.

By embracing the transformative potential that resides in every moment, we become the sculptors of our own reality.

Self-reinvention is not just a choice, it is an act of courage, intention and continual growth.

By making this choice, we open the door to a fulfilling reality and a future filled with endless possibilities.

Chapitre 2
Planting the Seeds of Change

Imagine yourself as a seed being planted in the fertile soil of your own reality. In this chapter, we will dive deeper into the concept of personal growth by exploring the essential steps to cultivate your transformation. You will discover how to identify your deepest desires, those waiting to be nurtured to blossom and guide you towards a fulfilling future.

Through hands-on exercises and deep reflections, you'll learn how to define your goals in meaningful ways and establish a solid foundation for your journey of reinvention.

I also invite you to explore the **roots of your identity** , to challenge limiting beliefs that may be hindering your growth, and to open yourself to new perspectives.

Just as a seed needs light and water to grow, you will learn how to nurture your mind and soul with the elements necessary to thrive.

Imagine yourself as a gardener of your own reality. You have the power to sow seeds that will give birth to future experiences and results.

In this chapter we will also explore how to consciously choose the seeds you plant and how to cultivate the habits that support your personal transformation.

The Interior Garden

Think of your mind as an inner garden.
The thoughts, beliefs and emotions you harbor are the seeds you plant in this garden.
However, it is easy to let negative and limiting seeds take root.
Identify these seeds and replace them with ones that promote growth.

✦ Cultivate Self-Awareness

The first step to reinventing your reality is to cultivate self-awareness. Take the time to observe yourself, identify the thought patterns and beliefs that are holding you back.

- Ask yourself deep questions:

"What thoughts limit me?", "What beliefs no longer serve me?"

Self-awareness is the key to digging up negative seeds and replacing them with positive seeds.

✦ Choose Your Seeds Carefully

Once you've identified the negative seeds, it's time to consciously replace them.

Choose the seeds of positive thinking, self-confidence and possibility.

For example, if you tend to criticize yourself, replace this seed with the affirmation: "I am worthy of love and success."

✦ Cultivate Habits of Transformation

The seeds you plant must be watered and nurtured to grow.
This is where habits come in. Identify the habits that support your personal transformation.

Perhaps meditation, exercise, inspirational reading, or gratitude are among those habits.
Create a plan to consciously integrate them into your daily life.

✦ Overcome Obstacles

Every gardener and every gardener encounters obstacles, such as weeds that threaten to take over.

In your inner garden, these obstacles can be doubts, fears or moments of discouragement.
Learn to recognize these obstacles and deal with them with compassion. Use positive affirmations and visualizations to overcome them.

✦ The Power of Patience

Growth takes time.

Just as a seed does not become a tree overnight, personal transformation requires patience.

Be kind to yourself when you encounter moments of stagnation.

*Remember that every little sprout
of growth is a step towards a more
fulfilling reality.*

✦ Cultivate Gratitude for Growth

Gratitude is the fertilizer of your inner garden.

By acknowledging and celebrating every little progress, you encourage your personal growth.

Take a moment each day to express gratitude to yourself and to the transformational process you have undertaken.

Every seed you plant in the garden of your mind has the potential to blossom into future experiences and realities.

By cultivating self-awareness, choosing your seeds carefully, and nurturing habits of transformation, you create a fertile environment for your personal growth.

Remember, as the gardener of your reality, you have the power to create an inner landscape that reflects your full potential.

Cultivate Your Transformation

Essential Steps

Personal transformation is an exciting journey that requires deliberate intention and consistent action. Just as a gardener cultivates his plants with care, you can cultivate your own transformation by following these essential steps. Each step will bring you closer to the fulfilling reality you desire.

🌿 Step 1: Prepare the Soil of Self-Awareness

Before sowing new seeds, it is essential to prepare the soil of self-awareness.
Take the time to observe yourself and identify the thought patterns and limiting beliefs that have influenced your reality thus far.

Ask yourself questions like, "What thoughts are holding me back?", "What beliefs are limiting me?"

For example, if you believe that you are not worthy of succeeding, it may hamper your ability to pursue your goals.

🌾 Step 2: Choose Your Seeds of Positive Thoughts

Once you've identified the negative thought patterns, it's time to choose some positive thought seeds.

Replace limiting thoughts with positive, powerful affirmations.

For example, if you struggle with self-confidence, replace doubt with the affirmation, "I am worthy of success and happiness."

🌿 Step 3: Plant the Seeds of New Habits

Cultivating your transformation requires creating new habits that support your personal growth.

Identify the habits that will help you reach your goals.

For example, if you want to improve your mental well-being, develop the habit of daily meditation.

Start with a few minutes a day and gradually increase.

🌿 Step 4: Water the Seeds with Consistent Action

Just as plants need water to grow, your new seeds require consistent action to grow.

Take regular steps to nurture your new habits.

If you want to improve your fitness, commit to exercising a few times a week.

🌱 Step 5: Remove Weeds from Obstacles

In any garden there are weeds that threaten to take over.

Likewise, obstacles may arise during your transformation.

Identify these obstacles, such as fears or doubts, and develop strategies to overcome them.

For example, if you are afraid of failure, practice visualization to build your confidence.

🌱 Step 6: Patience and Continuous Cultivation

Personal transformation takes patience.

Just as plants need time to grow, your personal growth takes time and perseverance.

Be kind to yourself and remember that every little progress is a victory in itself.

🌱 Step 7: Harvest and Celebration

As your new seeds grow, take time to celebrate your progress.

Every small victory deserves to be celebrated. This boosts your motivation and strengthens your commitment to your transformation.

By following these steps, you can intentionally cultivate your transformation and create a reality that reflects your full potential.

*Every day, every choice and
every action is an opportunity to
cultivate the garden of your reality,
to create a life that resonates with
your deepest yearnings.*

Testimony

How did I succeed in my life? Each step of the personal transformation process has been an incredible adventure for me.

When I started cultivating my own reality, I realized how much power I had to create the world I wanted to live in.

At first, the soil of my inner garden was cluttered with doubts and limiting thoughts.

I struggled to believe in myself and feel worthy of success.

However, by cultivating self-awareness, I identified these negative seeds and began to replace them with positive thoughts.

I consciously chose to display the affirmation "I deserve success" whenever doubt arose.

Planting the seeds of new habits was a defining moment. I decided to create a morning routine that included meditation, exercise, and gratitude.

These new habits have had a profound impact on my day, helping me stay centered and positive.

The biggest challenge has been overcoming the weeds of fears and uncertainties. When I found myself facing moments of self-doubt, I used visualization techniques to boost my confidence.

Gradually, these obstacles lost their power over me. Patience has been my constant companion.

I understood that transformation does not happen overnight, but that every little progress counts.

Every step forward, no matter how small, brought me closer to the reality I wanted to create.

And finally, the harvest has begun. I started noticing the changes in my way of thinking, feeling and acting.

The positive thoughts I had sown had grown, creating a mindset of confidence and positivity.

The new habits I had cultivated had strengthened my discipline and determination.

Today I stand in a blooming inner garden, where the flowers of self-esteem, gratitude and passion bloom.

Every day, I reap the rewards of my personal transformation: more authentic relationships, unexpected opportunities, and deep joy in the simple moments.

I encourage you to follow these steps with determination and believe in your own potential.

Every little effort you invest in cultivating your personal transformation brings you closer to the fulfilling reality you deserve.

Practical Exercises and Reflections

Cultivate Your Transformation

Now, let's take action with hands-on exercises and deep insights to set meaningful goals and establish a solid foundation for your journeys of reinvention.

✦ Exercise 1: The Dream Map

Take a moment to imagine your ideal reality in all areas of your life - career, relationships, wellness, creativity, etc.

- Create a dream map by drawing or pasting pictures representing these aspirations.

This visual map will become your compass to guide you towards meaningful goals.

☙ Exercise 2: **SMART Goals** .

Learn how to set your goals intelligently and realistically using the SMART method . Each objective must be **Specific, Measurable, Achievable, Real and Time-bound.**

For example, instead of "I want to get in better shape", set a SMART goal . such as "I will exercise for 30 minutes, 4 times a week, to improve my physical health within three months."

☙ **Exercise 3: Deep Questions**

Ask yourself deep questions to explore your motivations and aspirations.

Ask yourself:

- "Why do I want to achieve this goal?",

- "How does this goal align with my values?",

- "What obstacles might arise and how can I overcome them?"

The answers to these questions will bring clarity to your goals.

🌿 Exercise 4: The Letter from the Future

Write a letter to yourself from the future, one year from now.

Describe your transformed reality, accomplishments, and happiness. This letter offers a tangible vision of what you want to achieve and motivates you to persevere in your efforts.

🌿 Exercise 5: Conscious Engagement

Make a commitment to your transformation by taking concrete action today.

Pick one small action that aligns with your goals and commit to doing it every day.

For example, if you're aiming to improve your creativity, commit to spending 15 minutes writing or drawing each day.

Deep Reflection

The Transformation Foundation

Personal transformation rests on a solid foundation. Take a moment to reflect on your values, what drives you, and what you really want in life.

Creating an authentic foundation will guide you in setting goals that are in harmony with your deepest being.

By integrating these practical exercises and deep reflections into your journey of reinvention, you will establish a solid foundation for your goals and aspirations.

Every step you take brings you closer to the reality you wish to create.

Use these tools as powerful resources to direct
your personal transformation towards a fulfilling
reality.

Chapitre 3
Elevation by Exploration

Exploration is the engine of personal growth.

In this chapter, we will dive into the process of conscious exploration to expand your horizons and embrace new experiences.

Imagine that each step you take into the unknown is an invitation to discover unexplored sides of yourself.

You will learn how to get out of your comfort zone and overcome the fears that can get in the way.

By daring to explore unknown territories, you can discover hidden aspects of your potential and unsuspected opportunities.

We will also discuss how curiosity and constant learning can fuel your transformation.

By developing a discovery mindset, you will be able to embrace challenges with enthusiasm and grow through every experience.

At the heart of this chapter, you will discover how exploring the unknown can open the way to an expansion of your reality, thus leading you to unsuspected horizons.

Exploration is the engine of personal growth. In this chapter, we will dive into the process of conscious exploration to expand your horizons and embrace new experiences. Imagine that each step you take into the unknown is an invitation to discover unexplored sides of yourself.

Getting out of the comfort zone

Step by step

Getting out of your comfort zone is essential for exploration.

From realizing limits to identifying areas where you can expand your horizons, each step will bring you closer to the unknown with confidence.

To get out of your comfort zone, it is crucial to start with recognition.

- Identify those habits, situations, and comfort zones that keep you in a certain routine.

- Take a moment to ask yourself, "What areas of my life do I tend to stay comfortable in?"

-

Once you have identified these areas, choose one to explore.

It could be a skill you've always wanted to learn, an activity you've put off, or even a difficult conversation you've avoided.

Each step into the unknown brings you closer to significant personal growth.

Overcoming Fears

Exploration Allies

Fears can stand as barriers in your path of exploration.

We will look at how to understand and overcome these fears.

By turning fear into an ally, you can bravely step into the unknown and discover parts of yourself you never imagined.

To overcome fears, it is important to examine them closely.

Identify the fears that arise when you consider stepping out of your comfort zone.

-   Are they linked to failure, to the judgment of others , or to uncertainty?

Once identified, ask yourself:

-   "What's the worst thing that can happen?"

Often, by confronting these fears, you will realize that they are less frightening than you imagined.

Then turn those fears into allies by recognizing them as signals for growth.

Whenever you feel fear, remind yourself that it's a sign that you're stepping beyond your comfort zone.

> *Make the decision to face these fears with courage, knowing that each challenge overcome brings you closer to your untapped potential.*

The Art of Curious Observation

Curiosity is the essence of exploration.

We will explore how to cultivate a curious observation of your environment and yourself.

By asking questions, staying open, and challenging your assumptions, you'll be able to see hidden details and opportunities from a new perspective.
To cultivate curious observation, adopt an attitude of astonishment towards the world around you.

Ask yourself questions like "Why is this so?", "How does it work?" and "What are the different possible perspectives?"

Practice active listening in your interactions with others, genuinely interested in their experiences and perspectives.

Curious observation also extends to inner exploration.

Ask yourself questions about your own reactions, thoughts and feelings.

Challenge any limiting beliefs you may have about yourself.

By developing this habit of observation, you open the door to new insights and possibilities that you may not have considered before.

Techniques to Get Out of Your Comfort Zone and Overcome Fears

1. The 5 Second Rule: Act Fast

When you feel the urge to explore something new, act fast.

Use the 5-second rule: count down from 5 and take action before doubts overwhelm you.

This simple technique helps you overcome procrastination and get out of your comfort zone faster.

❧ 2. Gradual Progression: Little by Little

Exploration doesn't require massive jumps right off the bat.

Start small.

Set small goals to start with, then gradually increase the complexity and scope of your challenges.

For example, if you are afraid of public speaking, start by sharing your ideas in a small group and work your way up to larger audiences.

🌿 3. Positive Visualization: Prepare Your Mind

Before stepping out of your comfort zone, take a few moments to visualize yourself succeeding in the situation you are apprehending.

Picture yourself handling challenges with confidence and calm.

This mental practice prepares your mind to approach the unknown with a positive and constructive attitude.

🌿 4. The Exploration Journal: Document Your Experiences

Keep an exploration journal where you record your experiences of stepping out of your comfort zone. Write down how you felt before, during and after taking the action. By documenting your experiences, you can see your growth over time and strengthen your motivation to keep exploring.

🌿 5. The "What if...?" Technique : Change Perspective

Whenever you catch yourself thinking about worst-case scenarios, turn those thoughts into an opportunity for change.

Ask yourself "What if things went well?", "What if I succeeded?"

This technique allows you to redirect your attention to the possible positive results.

🌿 6. Progressive Training: Confront Your Fears Gradually

If your fears are paralyzing you, try progressive training.

Identify the situation you dread the most, then create a series of gradual steps to deal with it.

Starting with the easiest, work your way up until you've exposed the situation that scares you.

❦ 7. Research and Preparation: Reduce the Unknown

The more you know about a new experience, the less scary it will seem.

Do the research, learn the details, understand what you can expect.

This preparation reduces the element of the unknown, which can reduce anxiety and give you more confidence.

❦ 8. Deep Breathing: Manage Stress

When fears arise, practice deep breathing.

Take slow, deep breaths to calm your nervous system.

This technique can help you stay calm and centered, even when faced with unfamiliar or stressful situations.

Curiosity and Constant Learning: Fueling Your Transformation

Curiosity and constant learning are powerful forces that can catalyze your personal transformation.

By cultivating these qualities, you can open the door to new perspectives, improved skills, and continued growth. Here's how this process can unfold, step by step, along with key points to remember:

⚜ Step 1: Cultivate the Curious Mentality

Curiosity begins with an attitude of wonder towards the world around you.

Be open to new experiences, ask questions and challenge your assumptions.

This inquisitive mindset invites you to explore a variety of topics, even those that at first glance seem far removed from your current interests.

Key Point: Curiosity is the fuel of learning.

It pushes you to discover the unknown and to find value in every experience.

⚜ Step 2: Identify Your Interests and Passions

Explore your current interests and passions.

What topics intrigue you the most?

What activities excite you?

By identifying what turns you on, you can direct your curiosity to areas that resonate with your inner being.

Key Point: Learning is more effective and engaging when you pursue topics that you are passionate about.

⸎ Step 3: Seek Miscellaneous Resources

Look for a variety of resources to quench your thirst for knowledge.

Read books, take online courses, watch educational videos, attend lectures.

Expose yourself to different perspectives and ways of teaching to broaden your understanding.

Key Point: Diversity of learning sources enriches your knowledge and promotes holistic understanding.

⚛ Step 4: Set Learning Objectives

Set specific learning goals.

What do you want to accomplish with your new skills and knowledge?

Setting clear goals gives you direction to follow and a sense of accomplishment when you achieve them.

Key Point: Learning objectives help you stay focused and motivated throughout your journey.

⬡ Step 5: Integrate and Apply New Knowledge

Learning only has value if it is put into practice. Find ways to apply the new knowledge in your daily life. If you're learning a new skill, look for opportunities to use it. If you gain new insights, explore how they can inform your decisions and outlook.

Key Point: Learning becomes meaningful when you integrate it into your life, turning it into action.

Step 6: Stay Open to Evolution

Curiosity and learning are continuous processes. Stay open to your changing interests and passions. What excites you now can change over time, and that's a natural part of travel.

Be ready to explore new paths and adapt.

Curiosity and constant learning are the pillars of continuous transformation. By cultivating an inquisitive mindset and pursuing lifelong learning, you nurture your potential and grow as an individual.

Each new discovery, each skill acquired and each expanded perspective contributes to your journey towards a fulfilling and evolving reality.

Chapitre 4

Inner Metamorphosis

Like a butterfly emerging from its chrysalis, inner metamorphosis is a process of deep transformation.

In this chapter we will explore how you can free yourself from past limitations and blossom into your true essence.

Through personal development techniques and change management tools, you will learn to release the thought patterns and behaviors that are holding you back.

You will discover how to nurture inner resilience and develop deep confidence in your ability to overcome obstacles.

We will also discuss how meditation, mindfulness, and other mind practices can support your transformation by helping you stay centered and connected to your own essence.

By embracing your own process of transformation, you will begin to blossom in a way that resonates with your true nature, paving the way to a more authentic and fulfilling reality.

Like a butterfly emerging from its chrysalis, inner metamorphosis is a process of deep transformation.

Let's dive deep into this transformation, exploring the key steps and practices that will guide you to a new reality where your true essence can flourish.

Release from Past Limitations

Step by step

Inner transformation begins with the release of the limitations of the past.

We'll cover practical steps to identify and challenge the thought patterns and behaviors that are holding you back.

Start with self -reflection : examine your limiting beliefs and the narratives you've built around yourself.

- Ask yourself questions such as "Where do these beliefs come from?" and "Are they really true?"

Once you identify these limitations, practice letting go.

Visualize yourself letting go of these burdens, like releasing a balloon into the sky.

When you release past limitations, you create space to welcome new perspectives and new possibilities.

Nurturing Inner Resilience : Strengthening Your Capacity to Overcome

Metamorphosis requires resilience. We will explore techniques to nurture your inner resilience, helping you face challenges with strength and flexibility.

Practice visualizing yourself overcoming difficult situations with calm and confidence.

By developing this mental image, you strengthen your belief in your ability to resist and bounce back.

Gratitude is also a powerful way to build your resilience.

Every day, take time to write down what you are grateful for.

This practice connects you with the positive aspects of your life, helping you maintain a balanced outlook even when faced with challenges.

Meditation and Mindfulness : Connecting to Your Essence

> *Meditation and mindfulness*
> *are essential tools in the process*
> *of inner transformation.*

Guided meditation can be used to explore your inner world, observing your thoughts and emotions without judgement.

Mindfulness brings you back to the present moment, allowing you to savor each experience with complete attention.

The Art of Transformation : From Cocoon to Bloom

Inner metamorphosis is a subtle art of transformation.

By releasing past limitations, nurturing resilience, and cultivating mindfulness, you create space for your own growth.

When you embrace this process with commitment and openness, you begin to see profound changes in the way you live and interact with the world.

As you walk the path of inner metamorphosis, you emerge as an inner butterfly, spreading your wings to embrace an authentic and fulfilling reality.

Each step of this transformation brings you closer to your true essence, releasing you from past limitations and opening you up to a world of limitless possibilities.

By integrating the practices and principles of this chapter, you are ready to continue your journey to a transformed and elevated reality.

Nurture Inner Resilience and Cultivate Deep Trust

Inner resilience and self-confidence are essential pillars of inner transformation.

By following these steps and practicing these techniques, you can strengthen your ability to calmly overcome obstacles and blossom into your true essence.

⚜ 1. Visualization of Resilience:

Take a few moments each day to sit in a quiet place.

Close your eyes and imagine yourself facing a challenge or obstacle.

Visualize yourself overcoming it with calm, confidence and resilience.

Imagine yourself as a solid rock against the waves of adversity.

The more you practice this visualization, the more you will strengthen your belief in your own inner resilience.

⚜ 2. The Power of Gratitude

Cultivate a daily practice of gratitude. Each morning or evening, take a moment to write down three things for which you are grateful.

This simple practice reminds you of the positive aspects of your life and strengthens your positive attitude in the face of challenges.

By developing a mindset of gratitude, you subconsciously nurture your inner resilience.

⚜ 3. Revised Narration

Identify the stories you tell yourself about yourself and your abilities.

If these stories are tinged with doubt or negativity, take the initiative to revise them.

For example, if you say to yourself "I'm not competent enough for this", turn it into "I can learn and grow by engaging in this challenge".

This revised storytelling helps you build confidence in your skills and pave the way for growth.

⚏ 4. Affirmations of Confidence

Create positive affirmations that boost your self-confidence.

Repeat them regularly, either aloud or mentally.

For example, "I trust my ability to overcome obstacles", "Every challenge is an opportunity to grow" or "I am resilient and adaptable".

Confidence affirmations help you program your mind towards a positive and resilient outlook.

5. Conscious Experimentation

Actively look for opportunities to get out of your comfort zone.

Each time you take on a challenge and overcome it, you build your resilience and self-confidence.

Take note of your successes, no matter how small, and celebrate them.

These small victories are tangible proof of your ability to overcome obstacles.

6. Self-Compassion

Be kind to yourself when you face difficulties.

Instead of criticizing yourself, treat yourself like you would a dear friend.

Self -compassion reminds you that everyone faces challenges and mistakes, and this is an integral part of the growth process.

By following these steps and practicing these techniques, you will nurture your inner resilience and develop deep confidence in your ability to overcome obstacles.

Inner transformation is an exhilarating journey to a more resilient, confident, and fulfilled self, and these tools are your allies in reaching that state of transformation.

Meditation

Mindfulness and Mindfulness Practices to Support Your Transformation

Meditation, mindfulness and other mind practices are powerful tools to support your process of inner transformation.

By cultivating these practices, you can stay centered, connected to your essence, and ready to embrace the profound changes taking place within you.

Here are some details and techniques for incorporating these practices into your transformation journey .

🌿 1. Mindfulness Meditation

Mindfulness meditation is about paying deliberate attention to the present moment, without judgment or distraction.
Practiced regularly, it helps you develop an acute awareness of your thoughts, emotions and sensations.

When meditating, find a quiet place, sit comfortably, and focus on your breathing.
When your mind wanders, gently bring your attention back to your breath.

⚘ 2. The Exploration of Thoughts

One practice of the mind is to observe your thoughts without becoming attached to them.

Sit quietly and observe the thoughts that pass through your mind like clouds in the sky.

Don't judge these thoughts, don't analyze them, just let them pass.

This practice helps you cultivate distance between yourself and your thoughts, which can free you from limiting thought patterns.

⚘ 3. Active Listening

Mindfulness is not limited to formal meditation.

Practice active listening in your daily interactions.

When talking to someone, concentrate fully on what they are saying, without thinking about your response.

Be present in the conversation, absorbing every word and every nuance.

This practice strengthens your ability to be fully present in all situations.

🌿 4. Mindful Walking

Mindful walking is the practice of walking slowly and mindfully, paying full attention to every step you take.

Feel your feet touch the ground, feel the movement of your body.

During this practice, put aside thoughts related to the past or the future and simply be present in the present moment.

5. The Practice of Gratitude

Integrate mindfulness into your gratitude practice.

When you take the time to write down what you are grateful for, do so with full attention.

Deeply feel gratitude for each item you write down. It intensifies your connection with the positive aspects of your life.

⚘ 6. Creative Visualization

Use visualization to create an inner space where you can reconnect with your true essence.

Sit in a quiet place, close your eyes and imagine yourself surrounded by soothing light.

Visualize yourself expanding and releasing all limitations.

Feel the connection with your deepest essence.

⚘ 7. Managing Stress Through Breathing

In a stressful situation, take a few moments to practice deep breathing. Inhale deeply through your nose for a count of four. Hold your breath for four counts, then exhale slowly through your mouth for four counts.

This practice instantly calms the nervous system and brings you back to the present.

By integrating these practices into your daily life, you maintain a constant connection with your inner essence and strengthen your ability to stay centered, whatever the situation.

Meditation, mindfulness, and other mind practices guide you on the path to inner transformation, helping you embrace change and blossom into your true essence.

Chapitre 5

Lighting the Paths of Possibility

Imagine that every choice you make is a step along an endless path of possibilities.

In this chapter, we'll explore how to make informed decisions that guide you toward a more fulfilling reality.

You will discover how to develop a clear vision of what you want to accomplish and how to align your actions with your aspirations.

We will also discuss how to deal with the doubts and uncertainties that may arise when exploring new paths.

Let's dive into the concept of intuition and how listening to your inner wisdom can guide you to choices that resonate with your true essence.

By learning to trust your intuition, you can make decisions with more confidence and confidence.

Here's how you can confidently navigate through the choices before you:

Developing a Clear Vision

Clarity starts with a solid vision of what you want to accomplish.

Take the time to connect with your deepest aspirations. Visualize yourself experiencing the reality you desire.

The more detailed and vibrant your vision, the more it will guide your choices towards paths aligned with your goals.

Align Actions with Aspirations

Your actions are the cornerstones of your reality. Every action you take is a step towards your aspirations.

Every day, ask yourself the question:

-   "Are my actions today bringing me closer to my vision?"

When you act in alignment with your aspirations, you light the way to your desired reality.

Managing Doubts and Uncertainties

When exploring new paths, doubts and uncertainties may arise.

It's natural. Acknowledge these thoughts, but don't let them paralyze you.

Use them as learning and growth opportunities.

Ask yourself:

-   "What are these doubts trying to tell me?"

You might discover hidden fears that can be overcome.

Listen to Intuition

Intuition is the voice of your inner wisdom. Learn to recognize it and trust it. When faced with a decision, take a moment to connect with your intuition.

Close your eyes, take a deep breath and ask yourself the question.

Note the sensations, thoughts or images that emerge. Your intuition can often guide you to choices that resonate with your true essence.

Practice Confidence and Assertiveness

Self-confidence is an essential asset to make informed decisions.

Remember your past successes, times when you overcame challenges. Each experience has prepared you to face today's challenges.

Repeat positive affirmations to boost your confidence.

The more you practice self-confidence, the more confident your decisions will be.

Refer to Inspirational Stories

Stories of people who have succeeded despite obstacles can inspire you in your own choices.

Learn from the experiences of others and use them as sources of motivation.

Remember that every choice is an opportunity to grow and progress.

Practical exercises

This chapter provides exercises to develop your decision-making skills.

One such exercise is to write down your options on pieces of paper and then draw them out. Observe your reactions to each option.

This practice can reveal your deep preferences, even if they are buried in doubts.

Light Your Path

By exploring the avenues of possibilities that open before you, you are actively choosing the reality you desire.

By cultivating clarity, trust, and listening to your intuition, you illuminate your paths of possibility.

Each decision becomes an invitation to create a fulfilling reality aligned with your true essence.

Exploring Informed Decisions

For a Fulfilling Reality

Making informed decisions is an art that can transform your reality into a fulfilling experience aligned with your aspirations.

By mindfully navigating through the choices that present themselves, you can create a reality that resonates with your true essence.

Here's how to explore this process to light your way to a more fulfilling reality:

⸭ 1. Clarify Your Goals

Before making a decision, take the time to clarify your goals and aspirations.

Ask yourself questions such as

- "What do you wish to accomplish?" and "How does this bring you closer to your vision?"

The clearer your goals are, the more your decisions will align with your aspirations.

⸭ 2. Evaluate Your Options

When faced with a decision, consider all of your options.

Weigh the pros and cons of each potential choice. Consider your values, needs and desires.

Mentally visualize the possible consequences of each option.

This in-depth assessment will help you choose the path that is best for you.

✦ 3. Listen to Your Intuition

Your intuition is a source of inner wisdom. When faced with a decision, take a moment to connect with your intuition.

Close your eyes, take a deep breath and ask yourself the question. Note the sensations, thoughts or images that emerge.

Your intuition can often guide you to choices that resonate with your true essence.

✦ 4. Avoid the Rush

Avoid making decisions on the spur of the moment. Take the time to think things through and weigh all the options.

Haste can lead to choices that are not in harmony with your deepest aspirations.

Give yourself the chance to step back and calmly assess each possibility.

✦ 5. Accept Uncertainty

Informed decisions do not always guarantee a path without obstacles.

Accept that uncertainty is a normal part of the process. Don't let the fear of the unknown paralyze you.

Instead, see every decision as an opportunity to learn and grow, regardless of the outcome.

✦ 6. View Results

Visualize yourself living the consequences of every possible choice.

Imagine the emotions, experiences, and situations that would flow from each decision.

This visualization can help you intuitively feel which option will bring you the most satisfaction and fulfillment.

✦ 7. Trust Your Judgment

Your own judgment is a valuable guide in decision making.

Trust your skills and ability to assess situations.

Recall past times when you made wise decisions.

Each experience has prepared you to make informed choices.

By exploring these steps, you illuminate your paths of possibility. Every decision becomes an opportunity to create a reality that resonates with your true essence.

By developing clarity, intuition, and confidence in your choices, you shape a fulfilling reality that reflects your deepest aspirations.

Trusting your intuition can be a powerful guide in making decisions.

Here are some concrete examples to help you integrate this valuable resource and make decisions with more confidence and assurance:

🌿 Listen to First Impressions:

When faced with a decision, take a moment to connect with your first impression.

What do you instinctively feel?

Sometimes our first reactions are influenced by our intuition.

Trust these first impressions and consider them a valuable source of information.

🌿 When the Heart Speaks

Your emotions can be powerful indicators of what resonates with your intuition.

If an option fills you with joy, excitement, or peace, that's a sign that it might be the right path for you.

Likewise, if an option is causing you anxiety or a sense of unease, it may be a warning to heed.

⚜ Listening to Subtle Signs

Pay attention to the subtle signs manifesting around you.

Sometimes the universe sends synchronicities or coincidences that can guide your choices.

For example, if you have several meetings or discussions on a particular topic, it may be a sign that you should explore this path.

⚜ Meditation and Deep Reflection

Meditation and deep reflection help you calm mental turmoil and connect to your intuition.

Before making an important decision, take time to meditate or sit quietly.

Ask the question to your mind, then observe the thoughts and feelings that arise. Your intuition can manifest in these moments of inner silence.

Consider Your Body

Your body can also give you clues about what resonates with your intuition.

When considering an option, notice the physical sensations you experience.

A slight expansion of the chest or a feeling of lightness can indicate that you are on the right track.

Tensions or twitching sensations could signal that something isn't quite right.

Emotional Analysis

As you consider different options, take a moment to imagine yourself having already made that choice.

- How do you feel emotionally?

If an option fills you with positivity and excitement, it may be a sign of your intuition.

If an option is generating negative sentiment or resistance, that could be an indicator that it's not the best path.

The Diary of Intuition

Keep a journal of your past intuitive experiences.

Write down times when you followed your intuition and it led to good results. Also, write down times when you ignored your intuition and later regretted it.

By rereading these experiences, you strengthen your confidence in your intuition and learn to use it more effectively.

Chapitre 6
Forging Fulfilling Connections

The connections we make with others and with ourselves play a crucial role in our growth.

In this chapter, we will explore how to cultivate meaningful relationships that enrich your reality. You will discover how to connect authentically with others by practicing empathy, open communication and compassion. We will also discuss how positive interactions can inspire and support you on your journey of personal growth.

Let's dive into the importance of connecting with yourself, learning how to cultivate self-love and unconditional acceptance.

You will discover how exploring your emotions, your values and your deepest aspirations can strengthen your relationship with yourself.

By forging fulfilling connections, you will create a support network that encourages you to continue to grow and evolve into the best version of yourself.

The connections we form with others and with ourselves are the threads that weave the web of our growth.

Build fulfilling relationships

✿ Make Authentic Connections

Authentic relationships are based on openness, sincerity and empathy. Take the time to actively listen to others and put yourself in their shoes.

Practice empathy by seeking to understand their emotions and perspectives.

Be authentic in your interactions by sharing your own experiences and feelings.

⚘ Communicate with Overture

Open and honest communication is key to cultivating fulfilling connections.

Share your thoughts and feelings respectfully.

Listen carefully to what others are saying and ask questions to deepen your understanding.

*Open communication creates a
space where ideas and emotions
can be freely exchanged.*

⚘ Cultivate Empathy

Empathy is the ability to feel what other people are feeling.

Practice empathy by putting yourself in the other person's shoes and feeling their emotions.

It strengthens the bond by showing that you care about how they feel.

Empathy also encourages better mutual understanding.

⅋ Inspire and Support

Fulfilling relationships are sources of inspiration and mutual support.

Surround yourself with positive people who encourage you to pursue your aspirations. Share your successes and challenges with those who support you.

Positive interactions nurture your self-confidence and boost your personal growth.

⅋ Connection with yourself

Connecting with others begins with a deep connection with yourself.

Learn to cultivate self-love by acknowledging your qualities and practicing unconditional acceptance of yourself.

- Explore your emotions, values and aspirations.

The more in tune you are with who you are, the more fulfilling your relationships with others will be.

⚘ Practice of Compassion

Be compassionate to yourself and to others.

Compassion is an act of caring and understanding for each other's struggles and imperfections.

When you show compassion for yourself, you create an inner space where you can grow without judgment.

It also allows you to better understand and support others.

🌾 Cultivating Meaningful Connections

Identify the relationships that nurture your personal growth and invest time and energy in them.

Spend quality time with people who share your values and aspirations.

Meaningful connections inspire you to grow and become the best version of yourself.

By forging fulfilling connections, you create a web of support that encourages you to grow and evolve. By making authentic connections with others and with yourself, you build a network of relationships that enrich your reality.

Love, empathy, and compassion nurture these connections, creating an environment for your personal growth.

Make Authentic Connections

The Practice of Empathy

Making authentic connections with others is a rewarding endeavor that begins with practicing empathy.

Empathy allows you to truly connect with the emotions and perspectives of others, creating deep and meaningful connections.

Here's how you can practice empathy to cultivate authentic relationships:

⧉ Active Listening and Non-Judgement

When interacting with someone, engage in active listening.

Focus on what they are saying without interrupting or jumping to conclusions. Suspend judgment and be open-minded.

By focusing on their experience, you show that you are genuinely interested in how they feel.

⧧ Put into Practice the Perspective of the Other

Imagine yourself in the position of the other person.

Try to feel what they are feeling and see the situation from their perspective.

This practice allows you to better understand their emotions and show that you care about what they are going through.

For example, if someone shares a frustration at work, imagine yourself facing the same situation to feel their experience.

❖ Ask Empathetic Questions ❖

Ask questions that show you care about their emotional well-being.

For example, ask "How do you feel about this?" or "What concerns you the most in this situation?"

These questions open the door to deeper and honest communication, allowing the other person to share their feelings in greater detail.

❖ Validate the Emotions of the Other

When someone expresses their emotions, validate how they feel.

Use phrases like "I understand this may be difficult" or "It's okay to feel this way."

Validating emotions shows that you acknowledge and respect their feelings, thereby strengthening the connection.

✦ Share Your Own Experiences ✦

Share your own similar experiences if you have any.

It shows that you are not just a listener, but understand what they are going through.

For example, if someone is talking about their work-related stress, share a similar situation you experienced and how you handled it.

Practical Example

Imagine your friend sharing that he feels overwhelmed with his job responsibilities. Instead of just nodding, you could practice empathy like this:

You: "I'm so sorry to hear you feel like this. It must be hard juggling all these tasks."

Your Friend: "Yes, it's really exhausting. I feel overwhelmed."

You: "I understand how draining this can be. There have been times when I also felt like it was all getting too much. How does this affect your emotional well-being?"

Your Friend: "It stresses me out a lot. I feel like I can't handle it all."

You: "I can imagine how stressful this can be. It's important to take care of yourself during these times. Is there anything specific that would help lighten this load?"

Using empathy in this way shows that you care about their emotional well-being and understand their feelings.

This strengthens the connection and creates a space where he feels listened to and understood.

Cultivating Self-Love and Unconditional Acceptance

Techniques and Examples

Cultivating self-love and unconditional self-acceptance is an essential journey in creating a solid foundation of confidence and fulfilment.

Here are some techniques and examples to guide you through this profound journey:

1. Practice Gratitude for Yourself

Take a moment each day to express your gratitude to yourself.

Identify a quality, accomplishment, or character trait that you appreciate about yourself.

For example, you might say, "I'm grateful for my perseverance in pursuing my goals."

2. Be Your Own Friend

Talk to each other like you would a dear friend. Avoid harsh criticism of yourself and replace negative thoughts with positive affirmations.

For example, if you make a mistake, tell yourself, "This is an opportunity to learn and grow."

3. Practice Self -Compassion

Imagine talking to yourself as you would a friend in trouble.

When you face a challenge, tell yourself comforting phrases like:

"It's okay to feel this way" or "I'm here for me no matter what."

4. Visualization of Love towards Self

Sit in a quiet place, close your eyes and imagine yourself surrounded by a light of loving kindness.

Feel this light that fills you with love, acceptance and benevolence.

Visualize yourself enveloped in this unconditional love.

5. Listening to Your Inner Monologue

Pay attention to your inner dialogue.

If you find yourself being critical of yourself, take a moment to turn that thought into something positive.

For example, if you tell yourself "I suck," change it to "I try my best and I'm constantly improving."

6. Self-Love Journal

Keep a journal where you write down something you appreciate about yourself daily.

It can be an accomplishment, a quality, or even a small victory.

Review your entries when you need a positive reminder of your qualities.

7. "Three Good Things" Exercise

Each night, list three good things you did or felt that day.

It can be as simple as "I took care of myself by taking a break" or "I showed patience with a colleague."

8. Practice Self -Assessment

Take a moment each day to look in the mirror and say out loud something that you appreciate about yourself.

It could be about your looks, your skills, or your personal values.

9. Dance of Trust

Put on some music and dance like you're full of confidence.

Although it may seem strange at first, this practice can boost your sense of pride and well-being.

10. Positive Affirmations

Create a list of positive affirmations and read them out loud every day.

For example, say, "I accept myself as I am" or "I deserve love and respect."

Practical Example:

Imagine you made a mistake at work and you feel frustrated and disappointed with yourself.

Here's how you could cultivate self-love and unconditional acceptance:

- "I remind myself that everyone makes mistakes, and it's an opportunity to learn and grow."

- "I'm proud of my past accomplishments and how I overcame similar challenges."

- "I accept myself completely, including my imperfections. That's what makes me a unique person."

- "I forgive myself for this mistake and choose to focus on the lessons I learned from it."

By applying these techniques and adapting the examples to your own experience, you can develop a more loving relationship with yourself.

Cultivating self-love and unconditional acceptance will allow you to view yourself with kindness and support you on your journey to personal fulfillment.

Chapitre 7

Shine around the world

Your personal transformation is not limited to yourself, it can have a positive impact on the world around you.

In this chapter, we will explore how to shine through your influence and contribute to positive change.

You will discover how sharing your growth journey with others can inspire and motivate those around you.

We'll also cover how to use your unique talents and passions to contribute to causes you care about.

Let's dive into the concept of social impact and how even small actions can create a ripple of meaningful change. By integrating your personal transformation with your contribution to society, you can leave a lasting positive imprint.

By embracing the power to radiate out into the world, you will connect to a deeper sense of purpose and meaning on your journey of reinvention.

Here's how you can shine through your influence

⯎ Sharing Your Growth Journey

One of the most powerful ways to shine is to openly share your growth journey with others.

Share your challenges, your successes, and the lessons you've learned along the way.

Your personal story can serve as inspiration and guidance for those who are also looking to grow.

✦ Using Your Talents and Passions

Identify the unique talents and passions that drive you. By putting them at the service of others, you create a meaningful contribution.

For example, if you are passionate about art, organize creative workshops for young people in your community.

✦ Commitment to Causes That Matter

Identify the social or environmental issues that matter to you and actively engage.

Even small actions, like participating in local clean-up campaigns, can have a positive impact.

Your commitment shows that you care about the planet and others .

Spread of Positivity

Be a source of positivity and support for those around you.

Offer sincere encouragement and show gratitude.

Your positive attitude can spread like a wave of constructive energy.

⯎ Initiating Meaningful Conversations

Engage in meaningful conversations on important topics like personal growth, sustainability, or caring.

These discussions can open minds and encourage others to reflect on their own impact.

⯎ Participation in Collective Projects

Join projects or initiatives that aim to bring about positive changes in society.

The power of a group can amplify the impact of your efforts.

Practical Example

Imagine that you are passionate about educating children from disadvantaged backgrounds.

You could shine around the world by doing the following:

- Organize free educational workshops for children in your community, encouraging them to explore their creativity and potential.

- Share your experience and challenges in this area on social media and at local conferences. Your journey can inspire others to get involved.

- Work with other volunteers to set up an after-school homework program.

- Initiate conversations with parents, teachers and local leaders to raise awareness of the importance of education for all.

By integrating your personal transformation into your actions, you create an impact that goes beyond the limits of your own journey. Your outreach inspires, motivates and creates lasting positive change.

Reaching out to the world is a conscious choice to contribute positively to society and to use your personal transformation as a means of making a difference.

By embracing this opportunity, you create harmony between your individual growth and your collective contribution, enriching your journey of reinvention.

Use Your Talents and Passions

Contribute to Causes You Care About

Each of us has unique talents and passions that can be channeled to bring about positive change in the world.

Here are some concrete examples of how you could use your gifts and passions to contribute to causes that are close to your heart:

🌿 1. Passion for Music and Teaching

If you are passionate about music and education is close to your heart, you could organize free music workshops for underprivileged young people in your community.

By teaching music, you provide them with an opportunity for learning and creative expression.

❦ 2. Communication Skills and Interest in Human Rights

If you are good at communication, you could use your skills to raise awareness and advocate for human rights.

You could write articles, moderate discussions or even organize events to highlight human rights issues.

❦ 3. Artistic Talent and Concern for the Environment

If you are good at visual art and care about the environment, consider creating artwork that illustrates current environmental challenges.

These works could be exhibited in local galleries or used to educate the public about nature conservation.

🌿 4. Cooking Expertise and Commitment to Healthy Eating

If you are passionate about cooking and believe in healthy eating, you could offer nutritious cooking workshops to youth groups or low-income people.

You could share simple and affordable recipes to promote better eating habits.

🌿 5. Programming Skills and Interest in Online Education

If you are proficient in computer programming and believe in access to education for all, consider creating free online learning platforms.

You could offer courses on topics relevant to disadvantaged young people who have little access to formal education.

🌿 6. Passion for Hiking and Nature Awareness

If you like hiking and are concerned about protecting the environment, you could organize educational nature hikes.

During these hikes, you could make participants aware of the importance of preserving local ecosystems.

🌿 7. Graphic Design Skills and Support for Social Causes

If you have graphic design skills and care about social issues, you could create eye-catching visuals for nonprofit organizations.

Your designs could help raise awareness of the issues and mobilize support.

Each example shows how a specific passion or talent can be used creatively to contribute to an important cause.

When you align your personal interests with a positive intention, you create a meaningful impact and leave a positive imprint on the world.

Using your unique talents and passions to contribute to causes you care about is a powerful way to weave your personal transformation into the fabric of society.

By sharing your gifts with others, you inspire and be part of the change you want to see in the world.

Social impact

Small Actions

A Wave of Significant Change

Social impact does not always require massive actions to generate significant positive change.

Sometimes it's the small actions, when done with intention and persistence, that can create a wave of lasting change.

Here's how small actions can have a significant social impact, with techniques and a practical example:

Dissemination of Awareness

A small action, such as sharing relevant information on social media, can raise awareness of a social issue among a large audience. Use powerful facts, images and stories to spark interest and empathy.

Technical: Create engaging infographics or posts that highlight key aspects of a social issue, such as education for disadvantaged children. Use relevant hashtags to expand the reach of your posts.

Community involvement

Participating in local events or community projects, even small ones, can strengthen the social fabric and improve people's lives.

For example, organize a neighborhood cleanup to revitalize public space.

Technique: Mobilize your friends, family and neighbors to participate in a clean-up day.

Show enthusiasm and optimism to encourage participation.

Individual Support

A simple act of supporting someone in need can have a profound emotional impact.

When you listen to, help or support someone, you contribute to a culture of empathy and caring.

Technique: Take the time to listen carefully when someone shares their challenges.

Offer your support by offering a solution or simply expressing your understanding.

Sharing Personal Stories

Sharing your personal experiences can inspire and connect people.

Share how you overcame similar challenges that others might encounter.

Technique: Write a short article or personal anecdote about how you overcame an obstacle, such as overcoming your own fears.

Post it on online platforms or share it with your friends.

Influencing by Example

Acting in accordance with your values can encourage others to do the same.

Your positive attitude and commitment to positive actions can inspire people around you.

Technique: Be consistent in your actions and your words.

For example, if you promote eco-responsibility, lead by example by reducing your own plastic consumption.

Practical Example

Imagine that you are passionate about fighting hunger. You could have a significant social impact by doing the following:

-   Collect non-perishable food from your friends, family and community.

-   Distribute collected items to a local homeless shelter.

-   Share your experience on social media to encourage

-   Host a small fundraiser to support local hunger relief initiatives.

By using your limited resources strategically, you can create a meaningful impact by addressing immediate community needs while inspiring others to join the cause.

Small actions, when done with intention and determination, have the power to create a ripple of significant change in society.

Every action, however small, can contribute to a culture of empathy, solidarity and positivity, thus contributing to a better world.

Flourish in the Unknown

The unknown is a blank canvas on which you can paint your boldest dreams.

In this final chapter, we will explore how to maintain your momentum of transformation as you continue to evolve into the unknown. You will discover how to embrace change as a constant and adapt to changing life circumstances.

We will also discuss how to overcome unexpected challenges by using your inner resources and your ability to find creative solutions.

Let's dive into the notion of continuous learning and how to keep curiosity alive throughout your journey. You will discover how each experience, whether considered a success or a setback, can be an opportunity to learn and grow.

By embracing the unknown with an open heart, you will continue to thrive, explore new dimensions of reality, and create a life that fully reflects your potential.

Here's how you can thrive in the unknown:

✦ 1. Embrace Change As An Opportunity

See change as an opportunity to constantly learn, grow and reinvent yourself.

When you embrace a positive attitude toward change, you create space to welcome new, rewarding experiences.

Technique: Whenever a change occurs, take a moment to reflect on the lessons you could learn from it and the new possibilities that are opening up for you.

⚜ 2. Demonstrate Adaptability

Life is fluid and unpredictable. Develop the ability to adapt to changing circumstances with resilience and confidence in your skills.

Technique: Practice meditation or deep breathing to help you stay calm and centered when faced with sudden changes.

⚜ 3. Overcoming Unexpected Challenges

Challenges are an integral part of the journey of transformation.

Use your inner resources, such as your creativity and perseverance, to find innovative solutions when obstacles arise.

Technique: Keep a journal where you write down your challenges and the solutions you have found.

It will remind you of your ability to overcome adversity.

✦ 4. Cultivate Continuous Curiosity

Keep your curiosity alive by exploring new knowledge and asking questions about the world around you.

Curiosity opens the door to new perspectives and exciting discoveries.

Technique: Set a goal to learn something new each week, whether it's reading a book, taking an online course, or exploring an unfamiliar topic.

✦ 5. Learn and Grow from Every Experience

Every experience, success or failure, can be an opportunity to learn and grow.

Identify the lessons you can learn from each situation to improve yourself as an individual.

Technique: After each meaningful experience, take time to reflect on what you have learned and how it can help you grow.

Practical Example

Imagine that you have decided to change careers and explore a completely new field. You could thrive in the unknown by doing the following:

- Attend workshops and seminars to learn new skills and knowledge.

- Collaborate with mentors and experts in the field for advice and guidance.

- Accept challenges and setbacks as opportunities to learn and adjust your path.

- Keep an open and curious mind as you explore new facets of your new career.

- Celebrate your successes, big or small, to maintain a sense of accomplishment and motivation.

By embracing the unknown with an open mind and a positive attitude, you will continue to thrive in each new experience, creating a life full of discovery and achievement.

Thriving in the unknown is an invitation to continue exploring, learning and growing through each phase of your journey.

By demonstrating adaptability, curiosity and resilience, you transform the unknown into a canvas on which you can paint your boldest dreams, creating a reality that fully reflects your potential and determination.

Keeping Curiosity Alive

Cultivate Wonder Throughout Your Journey

Curiosity is a driving force that fuels personal growth and continuous discovery.

Throughout your journey of reinvention, cultivating wonder at the world around you is essential.

Here's how you can keep curiosity alive:

⧫ 1. Practice Mindfulness

Mindfulness allows you to live in the present moment with open and inquisitive attention.

By practicing mindfulness, you develop the ability to notice the subtle details of your surroundings and appreciate each experience.

Technique: Choose a time each day to be fully present.

Observe the sensations, smells, sounds and colors around you, marveling at the richness of your experience.

⟐ 2. Ask Questions

Never stop asking questions. Every situation, every interaction and every experience is an opportunity to learn something new. Be curious and open to constant learning.

Technique: Get in the habit of asking at least one question a day.

It can be a simple question, like "Why does it work this way?", which will inspire you to explore further.

⟐ 3. Explore New Interests

Do not limit yourself to your current areas of knowledge. Explore new subjects, hobbies and skills. Discovering unknown areas will broaden your horizons and open you up to new perspectives.

Technique: Regularly choose a subject that intrigues you but that you do not know well.

Do research, read articles or watch videos to deepen your understanding.

⬍ 4. Observe the Beauty of Nature

Nature offers an endless source of wonder.

Take time to contemplate the sunsets, the stars in the night sky, the textures of the leaves and the movements of the animals.

Marvel at the complexity of life.

Technique: Devote time each week to an outdoor activity, whether it's a walk in nature, a picnic in a park, or simply gazing at the sky.

⬍ 5. Experiment with New Perspectives

Develop your curiosity by changing perspective. Approach situations as if you were seeing them for the first time, being open to new interpretations and enriching experiences.

Technique: Imagine that you are an outside observer of your own life.

Look at your experiences from different angles to get new and inspiring insights.

⇟ 6. Keep a Discovery Journal

Keep a journal where you write down all the things that intrigue you, the new knowledge you acquire, and the questions you ask.

Reread these entries to remember how rich the world is with learning opportunities.

Technique: Set aside time each day to write in your discovery journal. Relive your moments of curiosity and wonder.

By keeping curiosity alive, you enrich your journey of reinvention by developing a mindset of perpetual learning.

Every day becomes an opportunity to experience something new, marvel at the beauty of the world, and enrich your understanding of yourself and your reality.

Overcoming Unexpected Challenges

Cultivating Inner Resilience and Creativity

Unexpected challenges are an integral part of life, but they can also be opportunities to develop your resilience and creativity.

Here's how you can overcome unexpected challenges by using your inner resources and your ability to find creative solutions:

⚘ 1. Cultivate Inner Resilience

Resilience is the ability to bounce back from adversity.

By cultivating inner resilience, you arm yourself with the strength to face challe nges with confidence and determination.

Technique: Practice positive reflection by focusing on your past experiences of resilience.

Remember times when you overcame obstacles and use those memories to build your confidence in your abilities.

🌱 2. Encourage Creativity

Creativity allows you to find unique solutions to problems.
By developing your inner creativity, you can turn challenges into opportunities to create something new and innovative.

Technique: Make a habit of writing down all the ideas that come to mind when you are faced with a challenge. Even the craziest ideas could contain useful elements.

❦ 3. Positive Visualization

Positive visualization helps you project yourself into a successful future despite current challenges.

By imagining your success, you build your confidence and determination to overcome obstacles.

Technique: Close your eyes and imagine yourself successfully overcoming the challenge.

Feel the positive emotions associated with your success, which will reinforce your positive mindset.

❦ 4. Use of Metaphors

Metaphors can help you see challenges from a different perspective and find creative solutions.

Associate the challenge with a metaphor that evokes resolution and growth.

Technique: For example, if you face an obstacle, imagine it as a closed door. By finding the key to open this door, you will be able to overcome the challenge.

⚜ 5. Creative Brainstorming

Engage in creative brainstorming by bringing together a group of friends or colleagues to discuss the challenge and generate ideas.

The exchange of ideas can open new perspectives.

Technique: Organize a brainstorming session where each participant comes up with at least three ideas for solving the challenge. Encourage free and uncritical thinking.

Practical Example

Imagine that you lost your job unexpectedly. To overcome this challenge, you could use your inner resources and creativity in the following ways:

- Challenge: Unexpected job loss.

Inner Resources: Faith in your skills, history of success, resilience.

Creative Solution: You decide to use this time to explore an area you've always wanted to explore. You start working on a personal project that showcases your unique skills and passions.

Positive Visualization: You imagine yourself presenting your personal project successfully to potential partners, which gives you a boost of confidence and determination.

Metaphor: You associate job loss with a new door opening to opportunities more aligned with your aspirations.

Creative Brainstorming: You chat with friends about your personal project and collect their ideas on how to develop it further. Their fresh perspectives inspire you in new directions to explore.

By combining your inner resources with a creative approach, you turn a challenge into an opportunity for learning and growth.

Every challenge becomes an opportunity to develop your ability to find innovative solutions and overcome obstacles with confidence.

A New Chapter of Reality

Congratulations !

You have gone through this guide that has accompanied you on your journey of personal reinvention.

You have explored the landscapes of possibility, planted the seeds of change, lifted your spirit through exploration, experienced inner metamorphosis, lit pathways of possibility, forged fulfilling connections, radiated out into the world, and embraced the unknown. Your journey of transformation does not end here, as reality is ever-changing.

This book is designed to be a starting point, an inspiration, and a guide to guide you as you continue to evolve and grow.

Keep reinventing yourself, exploring new dimensions of yourself, and expanding your reality in a way that resonates with your heart. Remember that you have the power to unleash your full potential and create a life that reflects your deepest essence.

The journey to a fulfilling reality is an ongoing process, and each step you take brings you closer to the reality you desire.

May this book serve as your compass in your quest to reinvent your reality and unleash the full potential that lies within you.